money. Whether you're looking to build wealth, achieve financial freedom, or gain a greater sense of financial well-being, Christine Luken's masterpiece will surely guide you on your journey."

—Margo Bond Collins,
New York Times Bestselling Author

PRAISE FOR *PROVIDER MONEY PLEASURE MONEY*

"Christine Luken's book, Provider Money Pleasure Money, is a straightforward, enjoyable, and almost minimalistic approach to money. Any book that demystifies money and helps us find the balance we need in our personal financial lives is welcomed! I especially appreciate her mentions of the overwhelming religious influence on money. I wrote her sentence, 'Money's job is to support your happiness, not to be the source of it,' in my journal as something to remember and help guide me into a healthier relationship with money."

—David Hayward, the "NakedPastor"
and author of *Money is Spiritual*

"Christine Luken's 'Provider Money Pleasure Money' is a transformative guide that masterfully illuminates the energetic dynamics of money. This book helped me discern the distinct feelings associated with provider money and pleasure money, empowering me to embrace both with a newfound mindset. As a manifestation teacher, I've gained invaluable insights into managing and growing my own finances in ways I never anticipated. It's that good! Christine's wisdom and practical advice make this a must-read for anyone looking to enhance their financial well-being and manifest abundance in their life."

—Carissa Andrews, International Bestselling Indie Author
and CEO of Author Revolution

"Provider Money Pleasure Money offers a brilliant approach to personal finance! There is so much financial wisdom distilled into the classic energetic archetypes that pervade our world, making it easy to understand how, why, and where to improve your money management. Christine dismantles rigid, traditional approaches and brings a fresh, holistic view that is practical and accessible for our modern world. This book is such a gift!"

—Sarah Balmer, Modern Medicine Woman & Founder of Anchor the Light Mastery School

"What is money? While it's often viewed as a form of security, a scorecard, or an exchange of time, I prefer to see money as a form of energy. At its core, money is a transfer of energy, converting your efforts and time into dollars. This energy isn't lost but rather converted and stored for future use. Christine masterfully explains this concept throughout Provider Money Pleasure Money, offering a unique and insightful perspective on work, income, investing, and debt. Her approach will undoubtedly transform how you view and manage your finances."

—Robert Pagliarini, Ph.D., CFP®, EA
President & Chief Financial Advisor of Pacifica Wealth Advisors, Inc., and author of *Badass Retirement: Live with More Meaning, Money, & Adventure*

"*Provider Money Pleasure Money* by Christine Luken is a captivating exploration of our relationship with money, woven into an entertaining and enlightening narrative. From cover to cover, the author effortlessly draws readers into a world where financial decisions are not just about numbers but the intricate web of emotions and experiences shaping our attitudes toward money . . . With its engaging narrative style, insightful commentary, and actionable takeaways, this book has the power to transform the way you think about and interact with

PROVIDER MONEY

Pleasure money

The Energetics of Personal Finance

PROVIDER MONEY

Pleasure money

The Energetics of Personal Finance

Christine LUKEN

Provider Money Pleasure Money: The Energetics of Personal Finance

ISBN: 978-0-9985912-3-0

Printed in the United States of America

Disclaimer: Christine Luken is not a CPA, attorney, or financial planner. Please consult with the appropriate financial or legal professional before making major changes to your personal finances, taxes, investment, or legal strategies. The author, Christine Luken, and publisher, 7 Pillars, LLC cannot be held responsible for any outcomes, either positive or negative, as a result of the suggestions in this book.

Find out more at ChristineLuken.com

"Everything is energy."

— Albert Einstein

To Melanie,

Thank you for teaching duality and energetics in such a brilliant and understandable way.

Without your influence and belief in me, I might not have written this book.

It's for me, for you, for us!

To maximize your reading experience, download the Provider Money Pleasure Money Reflection Journal at www.ProviderMoney.com

Introduction

Although I got my one and only tattoo for my 21st birthday, I didn't truly understand the magic and meaning of it until almost 30 years later. It's a sun and moon kissing each other in the shape of a yin and yang symbol. As a teenager, I obsessively doodled the symbol in my school notebooks. I even had a black and white cat named Yin Yang in my twenties! I understood the concept of duality—having two parts with opposite meanings—on a surface level. It appears in abundance in nature: male and female, night and day, earth and sky, fire and water, winter and summer—two pairs of seeming opposites that complement and complete each other. We appreciate the characteristics of each half, especially in contrast with its opposite.

I didn't truly grasp the subtlety and enormity of duality until I spent significant time in group mentorship with Melanie Ann Layer in her Alpha Femme Experience. Suddenly, I saw the once-invisible web connecting and underpinning everything in my life. I jumped down the rabbit hole of the energetics of duality with both feet, and the veil lifted. I could see how these concepts ruled everything, especially money management. They were there all along; I just didn't have the right words for them.

Duality is ever-present in our money. There are two contrasting, yet complimentary energies that are the yin and yang of personal finance. In Eastern philosophy, the yin is passive, receptive, and nurturing. The yang is active, competitive, and productive. Discussions of yin and yang usually include mention of feminine and masculine energy. These energies should not be confused for male and female genders though. All of us have both energies of yin and yang inside us. Because of stereotypical gender roles associated with the discussion of the masculine and feminine, I refrain from labeling them here in our discussion about personal finance.

Money is gender-fluid! Or maybe a better way of saying it is that money transcends gender. It's neither masculine nor feminine, and it's also both. The energy of money contains both the yin and the yang. I refer to them as the Provider energy and Pleasure energy of money. Whether you identify as male, female, or gender fluid, your personal finances require a healthy blend of Provider and Pleasure energies! For the purposes of this discussion, I also use the words "money" and "energy" interchangeably.

This book is not meant to be a granular "how to" manual for your finances, unlike my previously published books. This is a philosophy of money and energetics. It's a paradigm you can adopt and adapt to fit your own personal philosophy of money. This book is designed to cause you to think differently about the entirety of your personal finances and how you relate to money. Once you have a solid philosophy of money, you can then more easily see the how-to pieces that you need to add or amend.

Are you ready to hop down the rabbit hole with me and see your money differently?

Chapter One

The Safety Net and the Swing

The dynamic of Provider Money and Pleasure Money is like the trapeze at the circus. For the trapeze artist to perform at his or her peak, two things must be present: the safety net and the swing.

If there is no safety net (or a badly damaged one), the trapeze artist risks life and limb. It's no longer fun or thrilling; it's downright terrifying to take a ride on that swing. If there's a strong safety net but no swing, there's zero excitement, which is the whole point of the trapeze.

The swing and the safety net are of equal importance. Having both is the only way a trapeze artist can have a truly enjoyable experience, feeling the thrill of swinging through the air, and also knowing he or she will be safe if a fall occurs.

The same is true with your money. In order for money to truly support your happiness, you need both Provider Money (the safety net) and Pleasure Money (the swing). To experience the full measure of happiness, it requires both security and excitement. Even if your financial resources are limited, you still can have a measure of pleasure in your money. But if your safety net is full of holes, your swing might be only a few feet off the ground, so you don't hurt yourself. When you build a strong foundation of Provider Money, your swing can be hung from the stars!

Chapter Two

Your Financial House

"Is your financial house in order?" You've probably been asked this question by a financial planner or tax professional. It's a polite way of asking, "Do you have your money shit together?" I love thinking of your personal finances like a house, especially as it relates to the Provider and Pleasure energies of money. Provider Money is the structure that supports the beauty of Pleasure Money.

Provider Money can be viewed as the building blocks of your financial house. It's the concrete foundation, the wooden beams, the drywall, the brick, and the roof shingles. These parts of your financial house might feel boring, but they are extremely important. Without them, the fun and the beauty are left unprotected.

When a house is constructed, the foundation, walls, windows, doors, and roof all must be in place before the interior decorator comes in with turquoise paint, an Italian leather sofa, and lemon-yellow throw pillows. We understand that the less exciting structure of the house is required to protect the whimsical flourishes of a home. If you decide to hang a gorgeous painting in your house before the roofer installs your shingles, it likely will get ruined by the elements.

The same is true of your finances. Provider Money supplies the safety, structure, and stability, so you can truly enjoy your Pleasure Money! However, if you build your house and furnish it with a card table and folding chairs, it won't be very enjoyable. Pleasure Money is the décor of your financial house: the beautiful artwork, cozy blankets, decorative hardware, and flowers on the kitchen table.

Pleasure Money includes the spicy and exciting things that make life memorable. For some people who are deeply in Provider energy, this might feel frivolous. However, money must support your happiness! Yes, happiness includes safety and security, but it also includes joy and excitement.

Provider Money and Pleasure Money are not opposites; they are complements. If you truly want to feel peaceful and positive about your finances, you need both. Crack open any personal finance book or tune into a money podcast, and you'll hear plenty of discussion around budgeting, debt management, emergency funds, insurance, and investing for retirement. This is the part of money that many non-financial people find to be boring and tedious. And it's very important!

If organization and financial management don't come naturally to you, don't worry. We all have the capacity for wise money management. What you might not have is the confidence or competency for it… yet. Two parts are necessary for financial competency: knowledge and practice. You don't know what you don't know. Your parents didn't talk about money. You never had the opportunity to take a financial literacy course. Well, you do now! You have a wealth of knowledge available to you at your fingertips: your phone.

Download a personal finance book, follow money influencers on social media, or subscribe to a personal finance podcast. (Head over to ProviderMoney.com for a list of suggestions to get started.) Once you have the knowledge and start putting it into practice, your confidence naturally increases. Money management is a skill, not a character trait! You wouldn't expect yourself to excel at snow skiing if you never tried it and didn't know any tricks or tips for how to stay upright on the slopes. Be patient with yourself as you learn.

Just because this part of personal finance is necessary doesn't mean that it has to stress you out or put you to sleep. The structure of your money can be a work of art, in the same way that you can build a house with gorgeous reclaimed wooden beams and a fieldstone exterior. Provider Money is never as sexy as Pleasure Money, but we can jazz it up and appreciate its simplicity and strength.

I'm a huge fan of creating pleasant routines around my Provider money in addition to automating as much of it as possible. Your Provider Money loves efficiency! I have as many of my monthly bills on autopay as possible. This ensures that I don't overlook anything or get hit with a late fee or finance charge. I also automate my savings and investing by setting up recurring transfers rather than relying on discipline to do it manually weekly or monthly. Just because Provider Money is all about structure, safety, and security, it doesn't mean it has to be stuffy.

The energy of Pleasure Money is like the décor of your financial house. Just as you would wait until the foundation, walls, and roof are finished to begin decorating your physical house, the same is true of your financial house. Imagine hanging a gorgeous oil painting by your favorite artist on studs without drywall or placing a $5,000 couch in a living room with no ceiling. We instinctively know the painting and the couch would be ruined without the proper protections in place first. In the same way, certain pieces of your personal finances need to be in place so you can truly enjoy your Pleasure Money.

I've witnessed people running up massive amounts of debt and depleting their savings for Pleasure Purchases like European vacations and ski boats, only to file bankruptcy and lose it all. Pleasure Money can only be truly enjoyed without guilt when we have a solid foundation in place. Now, this doesn't mean that we have zero splurge money while we are building and strengthening our foundation. Sure, buy that beautiful Moroccan throw pillow for your living room that's under construction. Just don't purchase an entire room full of furniture with the money that's earmarked to pay your homebuilder!

Pleasure Money adds whimsy, fun, beauty, variety, and excitement to your life. Life isn't meant to be all work and no fun. Unfortunately, some money gurus preach extreme frugality until you can check off all of your financial goals and pay cash for your next home. Being 100% in Provider Money energy for long periods of time causes burnout, which is why people rebel against those types of programs. Yes, Pleasure Money is frivolous, but it is also very important!

Chapter Three

Your Inner Provider King and Pleasure Queen

As glorious as the trapeze and financial house metaphors are, neither is sufficient for explaining the energetic subtleties contained in the complexities of personal finance. Enter the Provider King and the Pleasure Queen. They personify the energetic duality of money. The king and the queen complement each other and work in tandem to make your financial kingdom both secure and enjoyable. Let's pay them a visit, shall we?

Meet your inner Provider King. Every kingdom has a king. The king is in charge, and he ensures that the kingdom is protected from dangerous invaders and provided with the necessities of life. The king hunts, builds, fortifies, expands, strategizes, and protects. He focuses on the business of establishing, building, protecting, and expanding the kingdom. The king has both authority and responsibility. This is the Provider energy of personal finance.

Meet your inner Pleasure Queen. Every flourishing kingdom has a queen. A kingdom without a queen is more like a military stronghold, quite stark and unpleasant. The queen is cherished by, provided for, and protected by her king. The queen brings beauty, culture, and community to the kingdom. The queen also has authority and responsibility but is still subject to her king. This is the Pleasure energy of personal finance.

In chess, the queen is seen as the most powerful and exciting piece. She can move in any direction, for any distance. However, if her king is not protected, it's "game over." Although the king might not be as exciting, he is the most important piece on the chess board. When the Provider King and Pleasure Queen rule your financial kingdom together, there is a pervading sense of peace and prosperity.

Chapter Four

Money is Not Evil

If you believe money is evil or tainted (even a little bit), it will rob you of the enjoyment of your money. Money is a tool – a means of exchange. Money is the means to get what you want, the intermediary. It's not the end goal in and of itself. We can't eat money, live inside it, or fly to Hawaii on top of it like a magic carpet. We don't want the money itself, but the things and experiences it can buy, like a delicious meal, a cottage by the sea, or a plane ticket to the tropics.

So, how did this tool become so infused with morality, especially evil? Interestingly, the apostle Paul says in Timothy 6:10, "*The love of money is a root of all kinds of evil. Some people, eager for money, have wandered from the faith and pierced themselves with many griefs.*" As you can see, it's not the money itself but making it the most important thing in your life that leads to unpleasant consequences. I think we can all agree that our relationships, both with the human and the divine, should have a higher priority than a tool like money.

Money's job is to support your happiness, not to be the source of it. I like to think of money as my personal assistant or my employee. If I am a great manager of money, it will serve me well. If you put money on a pedestal, expecting it to be a magic genie who will transform your entire life when you accumulate a certain amount of it, you'll be sorely disappointed. The key is to build a beautiful life right here and now so that when the big money comes, it's like the rainbow sprinkles on your cupcake.

Unfortunately, society perpetuates the "money is evil" paradigm and takes it even further by casting rich people in the role of villains. How many movies and shows have you watched where the hero or heroine has a heart of gold (but an empty bank account), and their nemesis is wealthy, powerful, and cold-hearted? It starts in childhood with fairy tales and Disney movies. Do we hear stories on the news about millionaires and billionaires who are doing kind things and donating large amounts of money to charity? Rarely! But we frequently see headlines about the greediness of corporate CEOs and Wall Street investors.

I've heard people say things about ultra-wealthy people like, "No one should have that much money." The problem with criticizing rich people is that you're demonizing the very thing you (perhaps secretly) aspire to be. If, deep down, you think that being wealthy might corrupt your good character, you will unconsciously sabotage your financial success. Why? Because we all want to be "good" people.

Actor Will Smith said, "Money and success don't change people; they merely amplify what is already there." Deeming all rich people as evil and poor people (or people of modest means) as good is a form of prejudice. We all know someone who's poor and also an asshole. Being rich or poor is a variable that is completely unrelated to one's moral character. Untangling this issue is important if you want to have a healthy and balanced relationship with money!

Some religions advocate shunning money and taking vows of poverty. This causes people to avoid or ignore even their financial stability because it's not "spiritual." Many people believe that you can't be both spiritually rich and financially rich at the same time. We judge others who have more financial resources and how they use them. *"If I had that much money, I would never…"* There seems to be a public outrage against spiritual teachers who become wealthy and well-known while they are helping people grow spiritually. This has always confused me because helping others advance spiritually is some of the most important work on the planet! Shouldn't those people be paid extremely well for it?

I have followed and financially supported the work of Joyce Meyer, one of the first female preachers with a worldwide public ministry, for over twenty years. She's talked about how her ministry has been criticized (usually by other religious folks) for the financial abundance that flows in and back out to literally hundreds of initiatives around the world. People complain that Joyce Meyer should live a frugal lifestyle if she's "really a good Christian." They seem to ignore the fact that she's written over one hundred books in her lifetime, and much of her financial compensation comes from her royalties. It's okay for JK Rowling, the author of the Harry Potter series, to be a billionaire, but it's not okay for Joyce Meyer to be a millionaire. These same people are completely fine with entertainers like Beyonce and Taylor Swift singing and dancing in glittery underwear, earning hundreds of millions of dollars.

If we're not rich, we can console ourselves with the fact that "at least I'm a good person." This lets us off the hook for facing the root of what's keeping us in financial struggle, both the mindset and the practical actions. *How much money are you allowed to have and still be a good person?* The question can't be answered precisely, can it? It's usually a little more than what you're making right now. We can choose to view wealthy people as proof that we live in an abundant universe. Will you see others as a trigger or a catalyst for growth and inspiration? The choice is yours! If you cast money as a villain in your life story, it will be difficult to feel positive and peaceful about your finances.

Chapter Five

Getting your Financial Kingdom in Order

Imagine walking into a grand castle, and as you pass through the gate, you notice random piles of garbage in the courtyard. As you enter the Great Hall, you see stacks of dirty plates and half-full goblets scattered on the tables. The inner chamber looks like a teenage boy's bedroom, not that of a noble king. You'd be shocked to see a royal castle so messy and unkempt.

The very first step to aligning with your Provider King energy is getting your financial kingdom in order, a.k.a. getting organized. The Provider energy of money is all about structure, systems, and order. If your accounts are scattered all over the place and your financial paperwork is a mess, it can cause feelings of unworthiness, stress, and anxiety. Disorganization can lead to avoidance of your personal finances, which costs you actual dollars in the form of late fees, forgotten subscriptions, and mindless spending.

It's time to channel your inner Provider King and take authority over your financial kingdom. Getting and staying organized doesn't have to be hard or complicated, but it doesn't happen by itself. I recommend setting aside 15 distraction-free minutes a day to complete the tasks in this chapter. In less than a week, your finances will be neatly tidied up, and you'll feel a huge sense of relief and accomplishment.

The first step to getting your financial house in order is to find all of your money. A king visits his treasury room regularly and takes stock of his gold, silver, and other treasures. A capable king knows the state of his financial affairs. For you, this means tracking down all of your accounts like a king hunting with a falcon. Find and document all of your bank accounts (savings, checking, money market, and CDs), retirement and investment accounts (401k, 403b, SEP, regular or Roth IRAs, crypto and brokerage accounts), cash apps (PayPal, Venmo, Apple Cash, Zelle, etc.), money owed to you by people or companies, uncashed credit card rewards, uncashed checks, and actual physical money including dollar bills and coins.

Be your own royal scribe and document everything either on paper or digitally so you can see all of your money. (Want a resource designed specifically for this?

You'll find it inside my Financial Tidy Up Bundle: www.tidymoneybundle.com) Did you discover money that surprised you? It's not uncommon for my clients and course students to find hundreds, even thousands, of dollars they didn't even know they had!

The second step to getting your financial kingdom in order is to declutter and streamline your money. Bring any money you found into your primary checking or savings account by cashing in rewards, transferring cash app balances, and depositing cash or checks. You might realize it's time to close certain accounts and consolidate. If you have an account with a small balance at a bank you rarely go to, close it out and deposit the money at your main bank. Don't hang on to accounts or credit cards solely for sentimental reasons.

Every account should have a specific purpose, so there's no magic number for how many you should have. I do recommend at least three: a checking account for all of your monthly expenses, a high-yield savings or money market account for your e-fund (emergency fund), and a savings account for your bigger Pleasure purchases. You might want to have two checking accounts, one for your Provider spending and another one for your Pleasure spending. The point is to remove any unnecessary accounts and proactively manage the ones that remain.

If you have "orphaned" retirement accounts (old 401ks that are still with a former employer's plan), recruit the assistance of a financial planner to roll them over into an IRA account that he or she can help you actively manage. If you don't already have a financial planner, feel free to reach out to my team at ChristineLuken.com for a recommendation.

Toss out any financial paperwork you don't need, like old insurance policies, expired warranties, bank and credit card statements from last year, etc. Much of the important financial paperwork you need can be stored electronically, so there's no need to be buried under a mountain of receipts. Talk to your tax professional regarding which financial paperwork you must save for your business and personal taxes, and shred the rest. Not long ago, I took 10 years of old tax returns to the office supply store for shredding!

The final step to getting your royal financial house in order is to spruce it up so your money feels at home. This involves adding anything that is going to make managing your money going forward easier and more pleasant. You might discover that your money's actual home is shabby and decide to purchase a new red leather wallet that makes you smile every time pull it out. This could also involve signing up for a personal finance app so you can see all of your bank accounts, credit cards, loans, and investments all in one place. If you want to save and invest more money, set up automatic transfers to those accounts.

If you feel yourself getting stuck or overwhelmed with this task, hire a financial coach to help you get organized and create a plan to move forward. Yes, even the Provider King is wise enough to hire someone who can help him achieve his goals quickly.

Chapter Six

Target Setting and Tracking Spending

The sun is rising through the mist of the rolling hills and surrounding forest. You hear the gentle hoofbeats of the approaching hunting party. The king's eyes squint and focus on movement in the brush. He pulls an arrow from his quiver and nocks it in his longbow. Like a King on a hunt for wild boar, you are tracking down rouge expenses and picking them off, one by one. Tracking your money is essential if you desire to be financially prosperous. Your money situation doesn't improve by accident. It improves with intention and action. Setting targets and tracking your financial progress is your Provider King's job, and he does it well.

Target setting and tracking doesn't have to be tedious or boring. I want you to think beyond traditional budgets and your preconceived notions about them. I teach my clients to embrace the Prosperity Plan as a superior alternative to budgeting. How is a Prosperity Plan different from a budget? Budgets focus solely on income and spending. Your income goes at the top, expenses are subtracted, and hopefully, there's a positive number left. A Prosperity Plan encompasses your income, spending, saving, investing, and financial protection. It is a holistic plan for your money that's focused on supporting your long-term happiness and well-being.

Most of us have emotional baggage connected to the word "budget." You might immediately think of unpleasant things like discipline, restriction, and no room for fun. Budgets are the monetary equivalent of a "Financial Keto" diet. I'm all for forward progress with your money, but going from one extreme to the other is the equivalent of "financial bulimia." If all you know is complete unrestraint with your money and you go on a rigid and frugal plan, you'll come to a point of burnout eventually. When you quit your super-restrictive plan, what do you do? You go back to the only thing you know: complete unrestraint. It's the same reason people quit low-carb eating plans – there's no room for fun!

One of my past clients, Allison K. Dagney, hated budgeting. She not only had emotional baggage but also unconscious drivers that pushed her away from the very thing that would ultimately allow healthy Provider energy to be present. Why did she dislike tracking and target setting so much? Allison's ex-husband watched her spending like a hawk. He scrutinized her receipts and restricted her access to the family finances. It wasn't uncommon for her to be on the receiving end of a lecture about spending too much on groceries or clothes, despite her frugality. Allison began to hate tracking her money even after her divorce because it gave her anxiety and made her panic. Although her ex-husband was out of her finances, his voice was still in her head. Her Provider energy felt more like a prison guard than a protective king! During our coaching together, Allison realized her emotions and unconscious conditioning around money perpetuated bad money habits that weren't serving her anymore. We worked on balancing her Provider and Pleasure energy, so tracking and target setting felt less like a prison and more like a roadmap to financial freedom.

The other reason I'm not too fond of traditional budgets is their black-and-white, pass-or-fail paradigm. When I'm coaching clients, I remind them that they haven't "failed" if they exceed one of their spending category limits by $100. When the personal finance app shows the category in red because they're over, it gives them flashbacks to elementary school report cards. It can be easy to feel disappointed or beat yourself up when you exceed your spending targets. *Get curious instead!* Did you go over it because you underestimated it? Or because a one-time event occurred? Also, you haven't "won" if you are consistently $500 under budget in a certain category either. It's more important to be accurate than to be under budget. Just like the king practicing his aim with a bow and arrows, your goal should be hitting the target as close to the bullseye as possible.

How much detail should you track? Should you have a category for every possible expense like electricity, water, trash, and internet… or a macro category like utilities? Is it okay to have a "miscellaneous" category? Some people love to see all the details, while others get overwhelmed by a myriad of individual categories. Step back and look at the big picture (macro-budgeting). Yes, micro-budgeting gives us valuable information and shows us where opportunities for change exist. When you first start tracking, you'll need to scrutinize the details to ferret out expenses that aren't adding value to your life. In the long run, we should be more concerned with macro-budgeting. Are you spending less than you make overall? Look at your income and spending over three, six, or twelve months versus a single month.

Another challenge with setting targets and tracking spending is that there is no such thing as a "normal month." Money experts tell you to take your annual expenses and divide them by 12 to arrive at your monthly expenses. Unfortunately, life doesn't work that way! Each month is going to be a little different. Most people's spending is 60-80% fixed and 20-40% variable. Many of your monthly expenses will be constant (mortgage, car payment, utilities), but some will vary wildly from month to month (healthcare, gifts, vacations). Use a personal finance app to help you estimate irregular expenses so you're setting aside money for them. This will prevent unpleasant "surprises" in your plan.

The Prosperity Plan is individualized, expansive, and flexible. It's not a Financial Keto plan; rather, it's more like the Mediterranean diet for your money. Yes, it's chocked full of fresh and healthy things, and there's also room for splurges. The Prosperity Plan contains a balance of Provider Money and Pleasure Money.

The key to setting financial targets and tracking progress is the weekly "Money Date." If you're single, you and Money will be getting intimate with each other, one-on-one. If you're in a committed relationship, it's you and your spouse or partner coming together to review your finances. Yes, I am asking you to have a ménage-a-trois with money! My weekly money date is a pleasant affair. I do it when I feel positive and peaceful, usually late morning on Saturday. I cue up one of my favorite playlists and bring a steaming cup of my favorite coffee into my cozy home office. I check my accounts, categorize my spending in my personal finance app, and pay bills. You might enjoy an evening money date with salsa music and a glass of sangria. I have a friend who dresses up in a ball gown and tiara with full hair and makeup when she does her taxes. How fun is that?

Go ahead, bring a little 50 Shades of Green into your money date. I once coached a couple who resisted the weekly money date habit. One found it tedious, the other boring, and both of them dreaded it. I made a bold suggestion: have a "sexy money date." I told them to come to their money date in their sexy underwear or even naked. The only rule was no touching each other until the money management segment was complete. Let's just say that I didn't have to nag them to spend quality time with their finances after they adopted the sexy money date!

Chapter Seven

Income

Provider Income

Provider income is steady and stable. It can be counted on to meet your security needs. Because it's not particularly glamorous, people don't get very excited about their Provider income. And that's okay, as long as you have gratitude for it! Your steady, stable Provider income takes care of the expenses that provide you safety and stability, such as your mortgage payment, utilities, groceries, and car insurance. Without this Provider income, we would be in a state of emergency and chaos. It allows us to create a comfortable financial home base we can relax into.

Provider income is any income that reliably comes in week after week, month after month. Salary from a traditional job is one of the best examples of Provider income. My husband currently works full-time as an industrial electrician at GE Aircraft Engines. His Provider income is as provider as it comes! His job classification is part of the union, so he is under contract to receive a particular rate of pay for several years. We know exactly how much my husband's paycheck is going to be week in and week out. We have designed our fixed expenses to be covered by his salary, even though we have additional streams of income that, some years, have been double or triple his salary. When your Provider income more than covers your Provider expenses, you can relax way down deep inside!

Provider income doesn't have to come from traditional employment. It's defined more by the fact that it is regular and reliable than its source. Other Provider income sources can include dividends and interest payments from investments, paying yourself a set salary from your own business, Social Security or disability payments, structured settlement payments, royalties, etc.

What if your income that pays for your Provider expenses isn't regular or reliable? If a big part of your compensation is commissions that come in erratically and in wildly varying amounts, that doesn't feel stable or steady. In my book, *Money Is Emotional: Prevent Your Heart from Hijacking Your Wallet*, I explain my method for taming the dragon of variable income in the chapter titled "The Income Roller Coaster." It essentially involves creating a Cash Flow Slush Fund account that you fund in your high-commission months so you can draw from it in your low-commission months. This artificially creates a smoothing-out effect to mimic having a stable and steady salary.

PLEASURE INCOME

Pleasure income comes without struggle and is received with joy and gratitude. You're being paid to be YOU. You're not being paid to work. This is usually money you don't need. Pleasure income is the result of you enjoying yourself, and the money "miraculously" follows. Although you might love your career that earns your Provider income, there is a distinctly different feel to Pleasure income. And the weird thing is that the harder you try to earn Pleasure income, the more you repel it. (That's because "trying" is Provider energy in nature.)

It's probably best to explain this with a story. I realized in Fall 2020 that I wasn't a gracious receiver. I often deflected compliments, turned down other people's offers to pay for things, and felt more comfortable in the giver role (which is Provider energy). I realized one of the things I love about being generous is having the other person receive it graciously. Because I was not a gracious receiver, I robbed other people of the joy of giving to me. No more! I adopted a new mantra for myself that's still one of my all-time favorites: "I am more than willing to receive ALL the money, gifts, and compliments that people want to give me." I began to write it and speak it out loud daily.

On January 1, 2021, my Dad asked my brother and me to meet him at his house for a "family meeting." I arrived a bit concerned because I knew both my Dad and stepmom faced health challenges (heart valve issues and lung cancer, respectively.) I wasn't prepared for what happened next. My Dad proceeded to tell us that his business was making more money than he could possibly spend in his lifetime. He wanted to transfer ownership of part of the company to my brother and me now so we could also enjoy the financial benefits. This meant that I would receive a percentage of the company's profits every year without lifting a finger. My Dad gifted us each a six-figure per year income stream with no strings attached. The only work required of me is to receive checks and deposit them when profits are paid out to the ownership team.

A few people would at least protest a bit. "No, no, that's too much. That's not necessary. You shouldn't have." But not me! Thanks to the repetition of my favorite mantra, I said, "Wow! Thank you so much! I was not expecting this. That's so generous of you." I embodied a joyful and gracious receiver.

You might be thinking, "Must be nice! I wish someone would give me a six-figure income stream." But can you even receive a compliment or a free cup of coffee from someone else, without protesting? If not, I hope you'll adopt my mantra and allow yourself to become an amazing receiver, too. Now it's also important to note that I have a proven track record of taking exceptionally good care of money that comes into my possession. I don't think this amazing gift would have been presented to me if I had been a financial trainwreck.

Sometimes, my Pleasure income flows in smaller and more sporadic ways. If I try a soft-as-butter face cream, listen to an awesome new song, or take a mind-blowing course, I tell everyone about it. I know this about myself, so if a company has a referral or affiliate program, I sign up for it. I'm going to tell people about it, so I might as well make a few bucks, especially if it doesn't increase the price for the other person. Last year, I received over $5,000 for telling other people about stuff I love! It takes almost no effort to sign up as an affiliate and even less effort to send a friend a link for the amazing face cream or online course I told her about over lunch last Friday.

Decide that you will be open to seeing easy opportunities to increase your Pleasure income. And not because you need it, but because it's delightful! Exercise your capacity to receive. Next time someone pays you a compliment, simply say, "Thank you." (Not, "Oh, this old thing? I bought this dress at Target five years ago for $15.") Want to take it a step further? Say, "Thank you, I receive that." You just might inspire someone to become a better receiver along with you.

Chapter Eight

Spending

Provider Spending

Provider spending pertains to your safety and security needs. It's the money you spend not because you want to but because it's necessary. This includes expenses like rent or mortgage, car payments, groceries, medical bills, insurance premiums, and debt payments. It can be easy to resent the fact that you have to spend money on these things. I'd like to offer you a different viewpoint.

Provider spending is taking care of you and making sure you are safe and secure. It's like the king of the castle ensuring everyone within its walls is well-fed, clothed, and sheltered. Without this spending, you are in crisis mode which means high levels of stress and fear. I experienced these feelings hundreds of times in my twenties when I lived with my ex-fiancé, Jeff. He was chronically underemployed, which meant we frequently didn't have enough money to pay all of our bills.

I distinctly remember the phone ringing (back when they hung on kitchen walls) and the bank's collection agent being on the line. He warned me that the bank would send a tow truck to get my car if I didn't catch up on my past-due payments. I felt a shot of adrenaline rush through my body. If I didn't have a car, I couldn't get to work, which would mean no money at all. It wasn't too many months later that I finally mustered up the courage to leave Jeff and get my life and finances back on track.

Since then, I deeply appreciate what my Provider spending gives me: safety and security. My needs are met, which allows me to engage with the rest of my life in a calm manner. How can you increase your gratitude for the Provider Money in your life? I discovered an amazing tip from Pam Grout in her book, *Thank and Grow Rich*. Whenever you pay a bill, write on it, "Thank you for the money!" It's an easy way to thank the Universe for meeting our safety and security needs. It's also a reminder to be grateful for all of the things we do have, while we're looking forward to the abundance that lies ahead for us.

Your Provider spending levels change as you move through various phases of your life and as your financial situation changes. A family with three children will have very different Provider spending needs than a young single person fresh out of college. As your wealth grows, your base level of Provider spending will (and should) increase.

Back in my twenties, I had no choice but to be super frugal, with Ramen noodles and generic pet food on my shopping list. These days, I spend money on organic groceries, monthly massages, and high-quality food for my fur babies, Marvin and Miley, which I consider to be part of my Provider spending rather than my Pleasure spending. These are part of preserving the well-being of my family and my health as I move into the second half of my life. I view these as part of my "routine maintenance." Now yes, of course, if a financial crisis occurred, I could certainly reduce these expenses, but it would cut into my feeling of security.

So, Provider spending isn't just the bare-bones necessities. It's the consistent payments for utilities, groceries, insurance, and housing that take care of you. When you look at your overall spending plan, usually 60-70% of the total is in the Provider energy. It's the level of those things that makes you and your family feel safe and secure.

PLEASURE PURCHASES

Pleasure purchases add spice to your life. They're based purely on desire and not need. And yet, they are essential to a healthy financial life. Money's job is to support your happiness. Once our safety and security needs have been met, we crave things and experiences that add beauty and meaning to life. Just as a Queen wouldn't care to live in a castle devoid of comfort or beauty, most of us don't want to live a spartan lifestyle with little enjoyment.

Pleasure purchases can be thoroughly enjoyed without guilt as long as we have taken care of our Provider spending needs first. If you get this out of order, you won't be able to experience the pure joy of your Pleasure purchases. I advise that even people of modest incomes set aside some money in their monthly spending plan for experiences and things that bring them joy. A Pleasure purchase can be as small as a chocolate bar purchased at a gourmet candy shop or as grand as an Italian sports car with red leather interior.

When it comes to Pleasure purchasing, I prefer to keep debt out of the equation. When the object of your desire comes with a monthly payment, it can sour your enjoyment. Years ago, Nick and I owned a wakeboarding boat that we thoroughly enjoyed. We initially financed the purchase but ended up paying the loan off in less than a year. Why? Because my husband realized that he resented the boat when he made the payments on it in the dead of winter while it sat in storage. The debt drained the fun out of our Pleasure purchase, and that was unacceptable. Since then, we have avoided using debt for any of our Pleasure purchases.

So, does this mean that you have to exercise delayed gratification for anything that's not Provider spending? I have an alternative to delayed gratification that I call Prolonged Pleasure. Here's how it works. Whether you have the money or have to save up for it, don't buy the object of your desire immediately. Instead, "flirt" with it. Look at it online. Visit it in person. Put a picture of it on your phone's lock screen. Daydream about the day you finally make it yours. By the time you purchase the object of your desire, you've picked out the perfect place for it in your home or office. You're excited to bring it home. Every time you see it, you appreciate and value it because it was a Pleasure purchase that you greatly anticipated, not simply an impulse buy. Here's an example of how I do it.

On my birthday, December 31, 2022, I stumbled upon a gorgeous painting in an art gallery in downtown Venice, Florida. It was a small seascape oil painting with quaint beach houses on the shoreline. I could have bought it then. I had the money to pay cash for it. But my intuition said, "Not yet." I snapped a picture of the painting instead. I told the gallery owner I'd be back for it on a future trip. I looked at my picture often, feeling deep down that this painting would be mine when the time was right. I didn't feel desperate for it or anxious that it might sell. Instead, there was a delicious anticipation for it, like a mature version of a child waiting for Santa.

Two months later, while back in Florida, I felt the pull in my heart to go and get "my painting." Not only was my painting waiting for me, but the price improved by $225!

The lesson? There is an art to spending money. When you spend intentionally, tuning into both your bank account and your intuition, there's nothing but pure enjoyment. It's like deciding to enjoy a single slice of gourmet chocolate cake, beautifully plated and each bite savored. This is "Pleasure Purchasing." When spending is an art, there is no bingeing, no mindless consumption, no regrets, no wasted dollars. Other financial gurus might shame you for spending instead of saving or investing. But spending is a beautiful and necessary part of the natural flow of money. I want you to discover the art of spending so that it's pure pleasure with no regrets.

Chapter Nine

Saving and Investing

Provider Saving and Investing

Saving and investing for the future is a prominent part of your safety and security in the realm of Provider Money. When you have adequate cash reserves for both expected and unexpected expenses, it creates a profound sense of safety and allows you to relax deep down inside. When you own income-generating investments that are growing over time, your anxiety about the future dissipates.

I want to differentiate between saving and investing here because, many times, they are used interchangeably. However, they are not the same thing. This is best explained by a squirrel and her acorn. (Weird, I know. But hear me out.) A squirrel collects and saves acorns in the fall so she and her little family will have food to eat in the winter. She is saving them to eat in the near future. When you are saving money, you are setting it aside to spend soon for a variety of reasons, like unexpected home repairs or a vacation.

If a squirrel were smart enough to invest, she would take a few acorns and bury them in the ground rather than eat them. If she did, five, ten, or twenty years down the road, the squirrel's ancestors would have tens of thousands of acorns to eat! But squirrels, unlike humans, don't live long enough to see the results of investing that far into the future. When we invest money via a retirement or brokerage account, we plant the money there and let it grow for long periods. We aren't going to need the "fruit" of that investment for many years. Pulling money out of investment accounts early is like ripping an oak seedling out of the ground to see how the roots are coming. You're not likely to get a good result.

The first, and usually least pleasurable, reason to save money is for unexpected expenses. This is usually called the emergency fund, or as the kids are calling it now, the e-fund. Saving for expenses we don't like to dwell on, such as a blown car engine or a job layoff, isn't exciting. Plus, you want to think positively, right? You don't want to dwell on negative things potentially happening to you because you might attract them. Ignoring the reality of financial emergencies is toxic positivity. You buckle your seat belt every time you get into a vehicle, don't you? It's not because you're rehearsing all the ways you could get into an accident on your trip to the grocery store. It's simply a smart move to protect yourself in case something bad happens.

The same is true for saving for unexpected financial expenses. Just as a safety belt gives you protection from the unthinkable on the road, so does your emergency fund when it comes to your money. It's the moat around the castle of your financial kingdom. We know unexpected "attacks" might come against our finances. An emergency savings account is a barrier that protects our daily finances.

When I lacked an e-fund in my twenties, anytime an unexpected expense occurred, I had the emergency itself (car repair, emergency vet bill, etc.) and I also had a financial emergency (how the hell am I going to pay for this?) Because I had no money in my savings account, I borrowed money to bail myself out of the crisis. I hurt my future cash flow by incurring high-interest debt to take care of that day's emergency. This led to higher levels of stress and anxiety. Now, fast forward twenty-five years, because I have plenty of saved money when an unexpected expense happens, I just pay for it. There's no drama! Sure, I might be annoyed that my car broke down or I need a new dishwasher, but that's just part of life, right? Financial emergencies are going to happen. The only unexpected part is when and how they'll happen.

Having plenty of money in your savings account gives you a deep sense of peace.

Here are several ways to make it easier and more pleasant to save money for unexpected expenses. Don't call it an emergency fund if you don't care for that term. Call it your "peace of mind account" or your "financial freedom fund." Just switching to positive language makes it more enticing to save. Who doesn't want peace of mind or financial freedom? Set up automatic transfers to your savings account a day or two after you normally get paid. Mindless spending will get you in trouble, but mindless saving will get you giant account balances! Automate your discipline using the "out of sight, out of mind" principle to your advantage.

You can also use negative emotions to motivate you to save for the unexpected. I coached a couple, Doug and Joanne, years ago. When they first came to work with me, their savings account balance was next to nothing. Whenever a financial emergency occurred, they would ask Joanne's mother for money. She always helped them out, but it came with a lecture and a heap of guilt and shame. Whenever Doug and Joanne had the choice to put money into their emergency savings, they would call to mind the aggravation of Joanne's mom's lectures and guilt trips. It motivated them to achieve their savings goals in a short time. For some, avoiding negative consequences can be an even more powerful motivator than achieving positive outcomes.

INVESTING FOR LONG-TERM GOALS

Investing is the epitome of Provider energy. You are providing for your future self's needs and wants. It can feel difficult to find the motivation to invest money for something so far off into the future. It's like starting to save for the $15,000 roof you know your brand-new house will need in twenty years. It's easy to procrastinate and deal with it later. Sure, you could get a home equity loan to pay for the eventual roof replacement, *but there's no such thing as a retirement loan.*

Time is your best ally when it comes to investing. The sooner you start, the more time your money has to multiply, which means you'll make more with less. If I could instill the habit in every eighteen-year-old of investing 10% for retirement, investment accounts would burst with so much wealth we probably wouldn't even need programs like social security for our elder years. So, what if you're way older than eighteen? What if you're thirty-eight, forty-eight, or fifty-eight? Is it too late?

Never! You will never be younger than you are today. And you most likely won't have the same physical stamina and level of health in your eighties or nineties as you do now. (Unless you take extraordinary care of yourself between now and then.) Chances are, you won't want to work full-time until the day you die. This means you'll have to invest some of your money now to provide for your future needs.

Retirement can feel very far off, especially if you're under forty. So, how do you motivate yourself to invest for such a long-term goal? An exercise I love to do with my clients is making "Elder You" as real as possible. We use one of the many apps with an aging filter to create a picture of what they'll look like at age eighty. Is it a little creepy and disconcerting to see yourself that way, with wrinkles and gray hair? Yes, and it should be. It's your job to take care of your elder self! Looking at that photo regularly makes retirement real to you.

But investing for retirement doesn't have to be a depressing endeavor either. Why not envision the amazing future you'll have in retirement? I recommend doing this with as much positive emotion and detail as possible. Nick and I want to retire to a tropical location, most likely in Southwest Florida. My father owns a house in Venice, Florida, so I spend almost two months a year there now.

I swim, play golf, and take long walks under the palm trees, which makes it a breeze for me to imagine what life will be like when I live there year-round. I know which beaches have the most beautiful sunsets and which restaurants serve the most delicious coconut shrimp. When I have a decision to make regarding investing for retirement, I simply need to recall my last round of golf or morning coffee enjoyed on my Dad's lanai, and I transfer money to my investment accounts.

Besides lack of motivation, the other reason people procrastinate on investing for retirement is intimidation. They're intimidated by the complexity of accounts, investment types, and tax implications. They're also intimidated by financial professionals who sound like dignitaries from a foreign land. I know because that used to be me, too. Despite having an accounting degree, I never received formal education on investing. I sought out experts and learned from them via books, videos, and real-life conversations. The good news is that you don't have to know everything about investing to get started. Your financial advisor will take care of the nitty-gritty details, but it's important to understand the basics. I've included additional resources with your Reflection Journal to get you started. It took time for me to fully embrace investing as an act of self-love. It's an important piece of Provider Money that I hope you'll grow to love as well.

PLEASURE SAVING AND INVESTING

Isn't saving and investing purely Provider energy? You might think so since it is an important part of your financial safety net. But we can also save and invest money in Pleasure energy, too. Since debt taints our pleasure purchases, we want to save up for the fabulous, fun, and frivolous things we want. People mistakenly think that saving and spending are polar opposites, but they're not. They are two sides of the same coin. You save money *so you can spend it later*. Provider saving is for the things you will need in the future. Pleasure saving is for what you desire to do or have in the future.

In the spending section, I introduced the concept of Pleasure Purchasing. Saving for those purchases is the other half of the equation. As you're flirting with what you want, prolonging the pleasure of wanting it, you're joyfully stashing away the dollars to purchase it. I highly recommend opening a separate savings account specifically for your big Pleasure Purchases. It's delightful to watch the balance climb in that account, knowing you're going to purchase something amazing soon, whether it's a luxury vacation to Costa Rica, a custom piece of 22k gold jewelry, or an original painting from an artist you adore.

Investing in Pleasure energy involves not needing that money *at all* for future use. In fact, if you bought an investment in Pleasure energy and it went to zero, your reaction should be, "Oh well! That was fun while it lasted." I don't recommend doing this until your Provider investments are optimized and fully funded for your future goals of retirement (and your children's education, if applicable). If you have excess money you want to "play with" and dabble in single stocks, day trading, or crypto, go for it. But only if you know you won't be upset if you lose all of the money. You can almost think of it as going to a casino. The goal is to enjoy yourself! And if you happen to leave with more money than you came with, that's a bonus.

Chapter Ten

Financial Protection

Provider Money is about safety and security, which means protecting against financial misfortune. I am a positive person. I don't spend much time dwelling on worst-case scenarios, especially when it comes to my money. I don't need to worry if the financial sky is falling because I have key pieces of financial protection in place: insurance, tax planning, and an estate plan. These things protect me from unforeseen catastrophes and worst-case scenarios, like thick, high walls protecting my financial castle from disaster.

Ah, insurance. We love to hate on it, don't we? It's a bill we pay every month, quarter, or year, and rarely see any "positive benefit" from it. Thank Goddess, we don't! Otherwise, it means we've totaled our car or lost our home in a tornado. Insurance transfers the financial risk we are unwilling or unable to take onto the insurance company. We're not taking a gamble that disaster will never come. Most of the time we are paying pennies on the dollar for the potential insurance benefit should tragedy befall us. Buying insurance to protect our income, possessions, and family isn't being pessimistic. It's being financially wise. I discuss the types of insurance you might consider owning in my book *Money Is Emotional*, so I won't rehash the details here. Talk with two or three insurance professionals to assess your family's needs and obtain competitive quotes.

Benjamin Franklin said that there are only two certain things in life: death and taxes. And these are two things we certainly don't like to talk about, so I'll be brief on both counts. Estate planning is one of the most loving, caring things you can do for your loved ones. Estate planning simply means you decide in advance how what you own and what you owe will be handled when your spirit leaves this earthy plane. When a loved one, whether your spouse or child, is surrounded by a cloud of grief, the last thing they need to deal with is a convoluted money mess. When our emotional volume is loud, it's difficult to make wise decisions, financial or otherwise. I've seen families devolve into chaos, fighting over a deceased parent's money and possessions. If proper estate planning had been in place, there would be clear direction and no room for arguing.

My stepmom, Francine, passed in 2021 from lung cancer at the age of sixty-two. She updated her estate plan a few months prior. My Dad knew her exact wishes and quickly executed them according to plan with very little difficulty or drama. What a gift! Healthy Provider energy in your finances protects and cares not just for you but also for your family. Please don't procrastinate on your estate planning, even if your financial resources are small. Once your estate planning is complete, communicate to your family what will happen at your passing so no one is shocked at your final wishes. It's important to review your estate plan every three to five years or whenever you experience a major life or financial change, such as marriage, divorce, purchase of a business, or birth of a child. Estate planning ensures your financial safety net will be strong and secure for your family when the time comes.

If there's one financial topic that elicits a collective groan, it's tax planning. The tax code here in the United States is so complex that there's an entire industry built around helping citizens navigate the labyrinth of rules. If you have any measure of complexity around your financial situation, it's a worthwhile investment to hire a smart tax professional. This will ensure that you pay exactly what you truly owe and not a penny more. I haven't prepared and filed my own taxes in over twenty years. I'm sure I could figure it out if I wanted to, but it's honestly not the best use of my time. (Plus, I got a D in Tax Accounting in college, so there's that.)

I recommend educating yourself on the basics of your taxes so you can have a coherent conversation with your accountant. This is especially important if you are a business owner. One of our largest expenses we rarely think about is taxes. Ignorance of the tax code will cost you money. There's a reason why people complain about the rich not "paying their fair share" of taxes. They understand the tax code (and hire professionals who do), so they only pay exactly what they legally owe and not a penny more. Wealthy people understand that certain investments (like real estate) and expenses (like those in a business) have preferential tax treatment. Reading Robert Kiyosaki's classic book, *Rich Dad, Poor Dad*, opened my eyes to the importance of tax planning. It's a wonderful place to start raising your financial IQ on the subject.

Chapter Eleven

The Energy of Debt

The energy of debt is quite different from that of income, spending, and saving. Debt, in and of itself, is a financial burden. It energetically ties you to the loan provider, whether it's a financial institution or a person. Back in Medieval times, if you didn't pay back what you borrowed to a person, you (and potentially your whole family) became that person's slave. When you enter into a debt agreement, you're obligated to repay the original amount plus interest. It's an immediate hindrance to your financial freedom. There's a reason we say someone is "weighed down by debt."

There's both a financial and an energetic weight you can tangibly feel when your debt levels are uncomfortable. Think of debt as dumbbells being attached to your financial safety net. Sure, a strong net can handle a few of them without ripping. However, if you have heavy dumbbells attached to your safety net, it might tear when it's supposed to catch you. Too much debt is certainly a financial strain, but it's also a physical and emotional one, too. Individuals who are stressed out because of debt are more likely to suffer from heart attacks, anxiety, insomnia, and ulcers. Releasing the weight of excessive debt is one of the best things you can do for yourself and your financial kingdom.

Before I hit financial rock bottom at age twenty-six, I lost sleep over my debt. Collectors called me constantly, my credit score tanked, and my anxiety was ever present. When I finally got my money shit together and began to tackle my debts, one at a time, I felt so relieved. Watching my debt balances go down month after month left me feeling confident about my financial future. Twenty-two years later, at age forty-eight, my husband and I paid off our mortgage, and we became 100% debt-free. I'm not sure I can adequately describe the deep sense of peace and joy, knowing that we own everything we have and don't owe a penny to anyone.

With that being said, I am not against you using debt in your personal finances. I'm simply advocating caution. You can use debt as a slingshot or a shovel. When you are borrowing for assets that increase in value, provide positive cash flow, or both, you're using debt as a slingshot. For example, let's say you purchase a duplex with a mortgage. You live in one half and rent out the other half. You use your tenant's rental payment to make the mortgage payment and pay extra on the loan every month. In time, your duplex is paid in full, has gone up in value, and is still providing you with a positive monthly cash flow. Like a slingshot, you take a step back into debt that, in time, catapults you into greater financial gain.

Conversely, let's say you are using a credit card to purchase expensive restaurant meals, concert tickets, and other things that have little to no lasting value. You're not paying the balance off in full, so you're accruing 20% or more in interest. That's using debt like a shovel. You're burying yourself in monthly payments that eat up your monthly income and stress you out.

The quickest way to ruin the Pleasure energy in your money is to bring debt into the mix. When you purchase the pleasurable things and experiences you desire with debt, it taints them with regret. Have you ever bought something you desperately wanted with debt and then later resented the payments? I think most of us have. Don't turn your relationship with Pleasure Money into a toxic one with debt.

Many years ago, I had a client who put a very nice, very expensive pool in his backyard. He used the financing company the pool vendor recommended to pay for it. He thought it would bring his immediate and extended family closer together to spend time enjoying the pool. The first year or two, they spent lots of time enjoying it. However, it didn't take long for the novelty of the pool to wear out, and it got used less and less. My client began to resent the pool more and more, especially when he saw the payment hit his account every month. What started as a joyful purchase became something he grew to resent for the drag it put on his family's finances. I'm not against buying a swimming pool; however, my client admitted if he had to pay cash for it, he probably wouldn't have sprung for it. The financing made it seem like an easy thing to buy (just $450 a month for the rest of your life!).

Debt is best used only in Provider energy for assets that care for your family, such as a mortgage for your home. There is a weightiness to debt that Provider Money can handle in moderation. When considering any kind of debt, be sure to count the cost, both financially and energetically.

So, what if you currently have debt dragging you down financially and energetically? First, be grateful for it. (No, that's not a typo!) Thank the debt for being there for you when you needed or wanted to buy something. Second, energetically release the debt and tell it you no longer need it. Third, make a plan to strategically pay it off as efficiently as you can. For example, my client with the pool might say, "Thank you, Perfect Pool Credit Company, for being there for my family when we wanted a pool in our backyard. I declare that your purpose has been served, and you can depart from our family finances." With this client, we determined refinancing his mortgage to assume the pool loan was the best course of action. We also tightened his cash flow up so he could make double pool payments toward the mortgage principal every month. He felt so much better about paying off the pool in this fashion.

Chapter Twelve

Giving and Receiving Money

Giving and receiving are halves of a whole. They're complements, not opposites. You can't give money without someone to receive it, and the reverse is true, too. Giving occurs in Provider energy, which should come as no surprise as you are providing the gift of money. Receiving occurs in Pleasure energy because there is nothing to do other than to allow the gift to be received. In a healthy giving and receiving exchange, the giver is excited to give the gift of money and the receiver is delighted to accept it. However, because money is emotional and people bring that emotional baggage into both giving and receiving, the energies can become tainted or unbalanced.

Have you ever said, "I'm just a giver! I love to give and I don't need (or want) people to give to me"? If all you ever do is give, give, give, and rarely receive, you can become depleted and harbor feelings of resentment. People quote the Bible verse Acts 20:35, "It's better to give than to receive," as proof of the virtue of overgiving. However, another translation puts it this way: "Giving gifts is more satisfying than receiving them."

I agree that it does feel amazing to give both money and presents to other people. It brings me great pleasure to see their joy in receiving. However, if we are unwilling to receive from others, it robs *them* of the joy of giving. Can you remember the last time you tried to give money or a gift to someone and they refused to receive it? Honestly, it feels pretty shitty. In rejecting the gift, it feels as if the person is also rejecting you. I'll bet you didn't attempt to give anything else to that person ever again.

If we love to receive money, but rarely give it, our Pleasure energy becomes stagnant. It's like the Dead Sea in the Middle East: water flows in but not out. And therefore, life cannot exist in its waters because they are stagnant. The Sea of Galilea, which isn't far from the Dead Sea, is teeming with plant and animal life. Why? Because water flows both into and out of it. We might have seasons of giving and seasons of receiving, but we want to actively participate in both.

Because money is emotionally charged, we might experience dysfunction in the giving and receiving exchange. This usually occurs between two individuals and not when you're donating money to an organization.

Let's talk about how this shows up and, more importantly, how to clean up our energy around it.

The first way unhealthy giving shows up is overgiving. My definition of overgiving is this: giving that violates your healthy boundaries or giving beyond what you can truly afford. Overgiving puts us in an unsafe place emotionally, financially, or both. I know from personal experience that this is a toxic dynamic. In my twenties, my ex-fiancé, Jeff, frequently pressured me to give him money beyond what was emotionally and financially comfortable for me. (I tell the full story in my first book, *Money Is Emotional: Prevent Your Heart from Hijacking Your Wallet.*) Overgiving left me broke, in debt, and deeply resentful.

Overgivers (like younger me) might develop a martyr mindset. *"I'm sacrificing myself for your comfort."* There can almost be a sense of pride and importance, a moral superiority of sorts. Overgivers frequently get their sense of importance by "saving" others from their financial emergencies. In therapy, I discovered that's called co-dependency. I essentially became Jeff's financial parent, and he was like my teenage son. Breaking this cycle was hard but necessary for me, and the relationship did not survive. Setting, communicating, and enforcing healthy boundaries around money in your relationships goes a long way in preventing this kind of unbalanced situation. (See the Reflection Journal for additional resources on healthy boundary setting.)

The other way unhealthy giving shows up is by giving money with strings attached. When we give money to others, it should be without attachment to how they will use it. Once the money leaves your hands, it's no longer yours to control. If we give money to someone so they can solve a particular problem or pay for a certain expense, we can become emotionally entangled in the outcome. If you know your brother's car is limping along, and he doesn't have the money to fix it, you might feel the pull to give him money. If you give him $1,000 and later find out that your brother found a mechanic who only charged $700 for the repair, are you mad he didn't give you back the $300? Or if your brother decides to put the $1,000 you gave him with his old car as a trade-in for a newer car with a payment, are you upset that he didn't use the $1,000 for the original repair? If you decide to give money to someone, and only for a specific purpose, it's usually best if you pay for it directly or don't give it at all. Some people, consciously or unconsciously, use the power of their money to control the people in their lives. If you know someone like this, it's best not to accept the gift of their money if you don't want the emotional strings attached to it.

Unhealthy receiving usually shows up in two ways: deflecting and receiving to the detriment of another. Deflecting occurs when you don't feel worthy of receiving and can be a sign of low self-worth. For some, their religious upbringing has conditioned them to believe that giving is morally superior to receiving. You might have been taught that it's not polite to be too eager to receive money or gifts from others, especially once you've outgrown Santa and children's birthday parties.

A story from my Dad's childhood illustrates this point beautifully. When my Dad was six years old, in the early 1950s, my Nana (his mother) took him to the doctor's office for a checkup and his immunizations. After the doctor gave him a shot and covered his arm with a bandage, he opened up a drawer full of brightly colored suckers. "Do you want a sucker?" the doctor asked in a thick Polish accent. In his shy six-year-old voice, my Dad answered, "I don't care." The doctor slammed the drawer shut and said, "You no care, I no care!" and left the room. Seventy years later, our family still laughs about the story. My Dad said from that point on if someone offered him something he wanted, he emphatically said, "YES, please!"

Receiving is a muscle, and if you haven't been using it, it's time to start flexing it. Pay attention when you deflect anything good: compliments, offers to help, gifts, and money. Honestly, even into my early forties, I found it hard to receive anything that I didn't achieve through hard work. It didn't seem fair for me to receive something I didn't "deserve." I noticed that I could barely even receive a compliment from a stranger without deflecting it. I finally decided that I was done with that, and I wanted to freely receive anything and everything the Universe wanted to give me. I adopted a new mantra that remains one of my favorites to this day: "I'm more than willing to receive ALL the money, gifts, and compliments that people want to give me." If I told you all of the money, gifts, and compliments I've received since adopting this mantra, you wouldn't even believe me. It starts with the little things. The next time someone compliments you, say, "Thank you! I receive that." (Then shut up! No deflecting or explaining allowed.)

Another unhealthy pattern is receiving to the detriment of others. This can manifest as helplessness or manipulation, or a bit of both. Usually, this type of unhealthy receiver can't seem to get their life together. Financial drama and money emergencies are the norm for them, and they rarely take responsibility for it. Excuses abound as to why the world seems to be always against them. Sometimes, people with these patterns are conscious that they're choosing to push their financial responsibilities onto another person. Others are operating out of their unconscious patterns, overwhelmed by feelings of self-pity and helplessness.

Unbalanced receivers find overgivers irresistible. Overgivers are their "knights in shining armor" who swoop in to rescue them. People with these unhealthy opposite behaviors are drawn to each other like magnets, as Jeff and I were attracted to each other. Jeff had the mindset that the world owed him something because he had a shitty childhood and his father was never there for him. There was always an outside source to blame for the problems in his life: his parents, his boss, etc. My nurturing nature kicked into overdrive, and I found myself mothering him both emotionally and financially. Because I had weak personal boundaries, Jeff easily manipulated me into doing away with them completely. What ensued was a seven-year toxic, co-dependent relationship that thankfully ended before the wedding.

At its core, the giving and receiving exchange is a beautiful and joyous part of our lives. To keep the energy as clean and balanced as possible, we must examine the motives we are bringing to the exchange. We can also trust our intuition when sensing the motives of others. For example, if your mother frequently gives you money, but then constantly reminds you of how she wouldn't need to give to you if you were more responsible with your finances, you can consciously choose not to enter into that exchange in the future.

The final thought I want to leave you with regarding giving and receiving is that you'll never achieve a perfect balance with it, especially regarding any specific relationship. In general, it's true that when we're generous givers, our generosity returns to us. But we don't give in order to get from a particular person. There might be certain people you give to who can never give money to you in return. God (or the Universe) rewards your giving, but you don't get to choose the conduit it comes through. By giving without expectation of when, where, and how much will come back to us, we keep our giving and receiving energy clear and open.

Chapter Thirteen

Generosity

We've already touched on the energies of giving and receiving, but I want to call attention to the beautiful energy of charitable giving and creating a generosity practice. I am talking about giving money to non-profits, charities, medical foundations, and religious organizations, not people. I first learned about the benefits of charity from my Dad shortly after I crashed and burned financially.

When he helped me create my first budget after I left Jeff and moved into his spare bedroom, my Dad insisted I give some money to charity. I argued with him that *I* was the one who needed a handout! He said, "When you're feeling sorry for yourself, just remember there's someone worse off than you who would love to be in your shoes." I felt like a failure because I had messed up my money situation despite having an accounting degree. Yes, it was a setback, but it wasn't the end of the world.

My Dad reminded me I had a roof over my head, food on the table, a good job, and a family who loved me. He suggested I begin my adventures with charitable giving by donating $5 a week to the local homeless shelter, Fairhaven Rescue Mission. Every time I wrote out the check to Fairhaven, I would thank God that I had food, shelter, and clothing. Shortly after I committed to giving $5 a week, wonderful "coincidences" started happening. A creditor was willing to settle for less to wipe out a debt. I received a raise at work despite my annual review being months away. It was like God showing me that if I helped others financially, He would step in and help me.

As my finances improved, I gradually increased my giving to a minimum of 10% of my income. Twenty-four years later, I still give money monthly to the homeless shelter, in addition to other charities close to my heart. When I feel like I can't afford to part with the money, that's when I know I need to invest it in others who are less fortunate than me. Regular generosity ensures we don't develop an unhealthy pursuit of and attachment to money. There are two types of generosity I recommend everyone engage in: continuous and spontaneous.

Continuous generosity is supporting a charity in an ongoing and committed manner. I treat these charitable commitments like any other monthly bill I pay. I like to think of myself as a benefactor who can be counted on to provide funds for the needs of the organization. Pick causes you care about, so it feels like a privilege to come alongside the organization to solve a problem, whether it's childhood poverty, curing lung cancer, or keeping puppies and kitties out of no-kill shelters.

Eight years ago, I sponsored a five-year-old boy named Angel from Nicaragua through Compassion International for $38 a month. Over the years, Angel and I have grown to know and love each other through the letters we write back and forth. The amount of money donated isn't much in the grand scheme of things, but my commitment to Angel is strong. If I faced financial hardship, I would cut every single fun thing out of my spending plan before I would ever stop sending Angel's monthly support. When you engage in continuous generosity over a long period of time, you develop a committed relationship with that non-profit organization and even the people who work in it. Three years ago, Nick and I pledged to support another young boy from Nicaragua, Jose. We are so committed to providing for "our boys" until adulthood that we've written Compassion International into our estate plan to ensure that happens.

I continuously support multiple organizations beyond Angel and Jose. Every month I donate to my local homeless shelter, a Cincinnati-based non-profit that aims to cure inner-city poverty with entrepreneurship (MORTAR), a local cat rescue, and several other organizations. I have also volunteered at most of these charities and thus learned exactly how they serve the community. It's good for us to be connected in this way with the organizations we financially support.

You probably guessed that continuous giving is Provider energy, and it's a vital part of a healthy financial plan. What isn't? Coerced generosity. If you are feeling external pressure or guilt to support any organization or non-profit, it's time to back away and reassess the situation. I've seen this happen to my coaching clients who have felt pressure to give, usually from religious organizations with no regard for the client's financial health or situation. Unfortunately, countless people have been financially and spiritually manipulated by church authority figures over the topic of generosity. Even I have been guilted into giving to various organizations over the years, and it's felt more like an encounter with a slimy used car salesman than the light, airy, and joyful experience it should be.

Many years ago, I attended a Christian entrepreneurship conference with one of my best friends, Heather. We enjoyed the speaker lineup and networking opportunities. Toward the end of the conference, we got ambushed by "coerced generosity." The auditorium lights dimmed as the video started on the massive screen in front of us. Without any warning, the video depicted stories of real-life child sex trafficking instances in other countries. It was both disturbing and heart-wrenching. As soon as the video ended, one of the conference leaders took the stage and pleaded with us to donate as they passed pledge cards with a form to enter our credit card information for ongoing monthly support. I complied and signed up to donate $50 a month. Whenever I received anything in the mail from the organization, I got an icky feeling, like I had been the violated one. This charity probably does amazing work with a global impact, but the way the church conference handled it felt sneaky and shady. I canceled my recurring donation after two years, and I felt immense guilt about it for quite some time afterward. Generosity is supposed to feel joyous. If it doesn't, just say no.

"The tithe" is taught as a spiritual principle in the Jewish and Christian religions. The word "tithe" means one-tenth. Multiple verses in the bible declare that a person will be blessed if they give 10% of their income "to God." In modern-day Christian churches, the message generally goes something like this. *"If you really love and trust God, you will give 10% of your income to your local church. If you don't see how you can afford to give that much based on your budget, just give it anyway because God will provide miracles if you put him first in your finances."*

If a person is already in major financial distress, putting another "bill" in their budget could cause other vital things to go unpaid. I've coached individuals who are behind on their car payments because of their tithe.

This causes them to be in a constant state of stress and nervous system dysregulation. The underlying message from their church is this: "You're not a good Christian if you don't do this. Don't you trust God?" Look, I want you to be so financially prosperous that you can easily give 10% or even more of your income and barely even miss it. Depending on your current situation, you might need to start at 1% or 2% with charitable giving and gradually increase it as your finances improve.

The other toxic thing I've witnessed is churches telling their congregation that the 10% they donate MUST go to their local church. This is usually substantiated by a Bible verse from the Old Testament that talks about the tithe going to the "local storehouse" that was overseen by the priests. Thousands of years ago, the church ensured that widows, orphans, and other unfortunate souls had their basic needs met. There was a single place where money was donated: at the temple. There weren't the multitude and variety of charities that exist in present times. Honestly, I'm a bit of a rebel, and I don't like other people telling me that I "have to" give them all of my charitable giving. I'm a grown-ass woman with intelligence, and I'll decide for myself which organizations I want to support financially. Feel free to do the same.

I've also had clients who feel guilty about decreasing their giving when their income is cut due to a job change or disability. One of my clients, Nancy, felt extremely guilty for having to reduce her church donations during a period of disability. For several months, she kept her donations at the usual amount despite a 40% reduction in her income. This put her in a negative monthly cash flow situation, where she tapped her savings account to "meet her commitment" to her church. We had a lengthy and tearful discussion about it, and she finally adjusted her donations to mirror her income situation and balance her budget. The beauty of giving a percentage of your income is that when your income goes up or down, your donations do, too. And yet, there's reluctance on the part of many churchgoers to decrease their donations when their income drops. It's usually due to the fear of what others in the church will think of them. I am giving you permission here and now: if your income drops, you can absolutely decrease your giving guilt-free.

There will come a time when you no longer feel aligned to support a particular organization. It's okay to stop. It's okay to decline when asked to give to a campaign. You don't owe anyone an explanation! In fact, I highly recommend that you review the organizations you regularly support at least annually. Are you still in alignment with their mission and the work they are doing in the world? Just because you're engaging in committed generosity doesn't mean you have to support the same organizations forever. Generosity should make you feel good, not guilty! Provider giving done right feels like a worthy responsibility, not icky, weird, or highly pressured. When you truly care about an organization and the work they do in the world, it's a relationship you feel committed to. And that's a very good thing.

The other type of giving I make room for in my spending plan is spontaneous generosity. This one has a ribbon of Pleasure energy threaded through it! In addition to my continuous generosity, I have extra funds available for the sole purpose of spontaneous giving. I know I'm going to give away the money in this account eventually. I don't know which person or organization will get it until I hear a need and get that zing in my spirit that tells me this one is it.

My friend and fellow personal finance enthusiast, James Lenhoff, first gave me this idea for what he calls an "Abundance Fund" in his book, *Living A Rich Life*. An Abundance Fund is a dedicated account for spontaneous generosity. The only certain thing about this money is that it will be given away at some point. James and his wife give the money to people in need as they encounter them and feel led to give. They each have a debit card on the account and don't need to discuss the giving of the money unless it's over a certain amount. "Guess who I got to bless today?" is a frequent topic of dinner conversation. How much fun is that?

Personally, I love to carry cash with me for spontaneous giving. I always have several $50 and $100 bills on me. I enjoy blessing people for excellent service at a restaurant or a friend who's going through a rough time. Giving spontaneously makes me feel like a fairy godmother, spreading magic and happiness everywhere I go. That feeling is well worth the money I part with, and I never ever miss it.

Chapter Fourteen

Too Much Provider Energy

I bet you know someone with too much Provider energy in their finances. It's the man or woman who is controlling, rigid, and obsessed about money all the time, even if they have plenty of it! When there isn't a healthy dose of Pleasure Queen energy, the financial kingdom is ruled by a tyrant of a king who immediately squashes any hint of merriment. Of course, it's wonderful to have structure and systems for your money, but they are meant to serve you, not enslave you. Are you a perfectionist when it comes to managing your money? Do you find it hard to lighten up and spend money "frivolously" without feeling guilty about it?

Financial perfectionism is a sure sign of excessive Provider energy. If you have numerous rules for how to manage your money or insist on doing things the "right way," you likely have an imbalance. If you're not sure, just ask your spouse or partner because they'll know immediately. If you've ever been called a scrooge or told to "just live a little," you probably lack a healthy dose of Pleasure energy in your personal finances.

My husband, Nick, has an abundance of Provider energy, which I found very attractive after breaking up with my financially irresponsible ex-fiancé. I love that Nick is an excellent saver who ensures we have a super-strong safety net. On the other hand, it can be difficult for him to loosen up and spend money on himself, even when he has an abundance of it. When Nick turned fifty years old, he decided to buy himself a mid-life celebration car. There was plenty of money in the savings account for it, but Nick spent three years laboring over the decision before finally buying his Lexus RC350.

Many times, too much Provider energy is present as a response to something negative from our past. I find many adults with this tendency grew up in a household where financial chaos reigned. When your life is full of upheaval because of money as a child, a natural response is to take hyper-control of it, even before you fully reach adulthood. This is exactly what happened to my husband. He lovingly called his mother a "hedonist." A hedonist is a person who lives for today's pleasure and doesn't worry about the consequences until they inevitably arrive. Nick and his siblings moved multiple times as children because of money or job issues with his mother and stepfather. He regularly overheard his parents fighting about the lack of money. It's no surprise that, as a teenager, Nick got a job and started saving money obsessively. These emotionally charged experiences can threaten a child's or teenager's sense of safety in the world. The brain encodes them in the body and unconscious mind to avoid them in the future at all costs.

The opposite can also be true. Unbalanced Provider energy might have been modeled for you by a parent, so you think that's the "right way" to manage money. If your mother or father controlled money with an iron fist, you might repeat that tendency, unconsciously believing that's the way it's supposed to be. Taking a look at how your parents spoke and acted with money is an important step to understanding your own financial tendencies.

One of the dangers of being in excessive Provider energy is the tendency to attract a partner who consciously or unconsciously wants to be taken care of financially. This sets up an unhealthy parent/child dynamic, where you are running around trying to clean up after your partner's money messes. This causes stress, tension, and resentment. Many relationships break up over money (more on that later), and this dysfunctional dynamic can be a major cause of it.

Has your financial advisor told you that you're on track with your investments, savings, and insurance, yet you still can't relax financially? If so, you might have an excess of Provider Money energy. Take some time to delve into your past and try to discover the root of this imbalance. Please refer to the Reflection Journal for tools to unearth and alchemize these triggers.

Chapter Fifteen

Too Much Pleasure Energy

Can there be too much of a good thing with Pleasure energy in your money? Oh yes, especially if there isn't a good dose of Provider energy to balance it out. If you have too much Pleasure energy, with very little structure or drive, your money will likely be chaotic and out of control. You no longer have the Pleasure Queen energy but rather that of a spoiled princess stomping her slippered foot, creating havoc in your financial kingdom.

Out-of-balance Pleasure energy frequently shows up as entitlement, disorganization, and financial drama. Bills are paid late, credit scores are low, and there's never enough money to go around. And yet, there's still money spent on concerts, lavish dinners out, and new outfits. You firmly believe if you make more income, your money problems will be solved. Unfortunately, that won't happen until you balance your money with a good dose of Provider energy. If you don't have the basics of Provider Money in place (like a spending plan and a healthy savings account), financial drama erupts whenever something "unexpected" crops up, like your annual car insurance premiums.

When there isn't a firm foundation of safety and stability, you swing between brief moments of bliss and long periods of financial stress. Either way, you are highly emotional about money all the time, whether it's terrible or amazing. These huge highs and lows keep you in a highly triggered state around money, which isn't healthy for your emotions. When your Pleasure energy is too high, you experience anxiety, which causes you to avoid dealing with your money. This becomes an unhealthy cycle because the more you avoid your finances, the more anxious you feel, and the more your money situation deteriorates.

Unfortunately, some people form unhealthy attachments in their relationships where they are codependent on others to be responsible for them with money. This is like the gorgeous yet helpless princess (or prince) who is in constant need of rescuing. This can show up as giving full control of your financial resources and activities to a romantic partner or even a parent. You might enter into relationships – whether platonic or romantic – with someone who is in unhealthy Provider energy. Not only do they take care of their own safety and security financially, but they take care of yours also. You're the person who needs to be taken care of financially, and this creates a lopsided power dynamic in the relationship. The responsible person is always bailing you out of your financial emergencies.

This is exactly the dynamic I found myself in with my ex-fiancé, Jeff. I had always been responsible with money as a teenager and had a little too much Provider energy, and Jeff found himself drawn to that. My excessive Provider energy allowed him to be irresponsible with money. He chronically underearned and overspent. He happily left the money worries to me, which created a toxic relationship dynamic, not to mention a disastrous financial situation for both of us. When I finally broke off the engagement, Jeff immediately attached himself to another woman who would take care of him. I'm not sure he ever learned his lesson. And if he can overindulge in the Pleasure energy of money and has a partner who will deal with the anxiety and drama, why would he?

Too much Pleasure energy can foster feelings of entitlement and little to no drive to earn or properly manage money. If parents don't start to delegate Provider Money responsibilities to their children as they transition into their teenage years, there's a risk they will never become financial grownups. They will either find a romantic partner who will be their "financial parent" or return to mom and dad for financial support. You and I both know people in their thirties, forties, or even fifties who have never grown up financially. Here's the thing: it's important for each of us to parent ourselves when it comes to money. We all have an inner child who has occasional irrational and unreasonable financial demands, whether it's overspending or a refusal to spend at all. We have to be mature enough to take control and not allow our inner child to call all the shots with money.

Chapter Sixteen

Barriers to Balance

Imbalances in your Provider and Pleasure energies typically stem from unresolved emotional money triggers, many of which have their roots in our childhood. I can (and will) write an entire book on money mindset and emotional triggers, but I want to give you a mini-crash course here. When we were born, we had zero opinions about money, either positive or negative. As we go through life, we collect opinions, experiences, and even traumas that create our "money blueprint," as T. Harv Eker calls it in his book, *Secrets of the Millionaire Mind.* By the time we reach adulthood, we each have a unique collection of emotional money experiences, both cultural and familial.

Unless a person is actively engaged in mindset work, they might not even be consciously aware of their money blueprint. The first major category of emotional triggers that causes imbalance is this: *What do you think about yourself having money and lots of it?* If your family, religion, or culture believes that having an excess of money corrupts your character, you might resist Pleasure Money as being frivolous and potentially dangerous to your morality. The last thing you want is to be one of those "evil, greedy, rich people." Someone with this deep-seated belief can unconsciously sabotage their financial success. Ask yourself, "How do I feel about possessing large amounts of money?" Does even asking this question make you feel uncomfortable?

Maybe you feel good about possessing more money, but the fear comes when you consider what other people will think of you. This is the other major group of emotional money triggers that trips people up: *What will other people think of me if I make and manage large amounts of money?* This can also cause you to put an upper limit on your financial success. I've witnessed people unconsciously demolish the foundations of their Provider Money to keep abundance at bay and therefore stay safely in their comfort zone of financial struggle. Ask yourself, "What am I afraid that other people will think or say about me if I am very financially successful?"

You know what is required to be financially healthy and successful, both in the Provider energy and Pleasure energy. Yet if "something" seems to be blocking you from achieving it with your money, you might have unresolved emotional money triggers lurking in your unconscious mind. Be sure to download the Provider Money Pleasure Money Reflection Journal to access the list of resources to further assist you with these barriers to balance.

Chapter Seventeen

Managing Your Emotions with Money

Money is emotional, and it's also logical. It's not one or the other; it's both! It bothers me when I hear financial experts say, "Just make the logical decision with your money. Leave emotion out of it." Why? It's because they're asking you to do the impossible – fight against the biology of your brain! The moment of decision occurs in the same part of the brain that also processes emotion. It's physically impossible to make a purely logical decision about anything, not just money. Those cool-headed money pros haven't left emotion out of their financial decisions, as they claim. Rather, they've trained their own emotions (whether they know it consciously or not) to feel good when they take wise action with their money.

There are endless ways that our emotions can wreak havoc on our money: emotional spending, avoidance, anxiety, fear of spending, or being a control freak. The key to making wise money decisions is consulting both the voice of reason (logic) and our emotions. Think of your logic and emotions as two radio stations playing simultaneously. The "Voice of Reason" station is like the classical music you hear in upscale department stores and elevators: low, soft, and consistent. The "Voice of Emotion" station is like a Top 40 channel on your favorite music streaming service: one moment, there's a loud thumping dance song by Beyonce playing, and the next, it's Ed Sheeran crooning a soft, sad, love song.

Your financial logic is like that "Voice of Reason" station. It's always there, quietly playing in the background. Your emotions are always there, too. Sometimes, they're so quiet you can barely detect them. Other times, your emotions are screaming at the top of their lungs! The problem is that you can't hear the Voice of Reason when your emotions are loud. Your logic is still there. It's just being drowned out by your loud emotions.

This is why I don't want you to make a major money decision (especially one not easily reversed) when your emotions are "loud." I'm not just talking about negative emotions, either. Have you ever made a financial decision in a moment of enthusiasm, only to regret it later? Let's be honest, we all have. Whenever you're interacting with your money, whether it's managing it, spending it, or talking about it with your partner, you want your emotional volume to be soft. The best financial decisions happen when you consult both your logic and your emotions.

Why wouldn't you want to disregard your emotions and just make a logical decision? Our emotions put us in touch with what is going on in our bodies. That's why emotions are also called feelings because the only way to experience emotions is to feel them in our bodies. There's a wisdom in our bodies known to us as intuition. Have you ever made a logical money decision that seemed perfect on paper, but you still had an "off" gut feeling about it? I know whenever I ignore my intuition (whether it's a financial decision or any other kind of decision), I always end up regretting it. It's about balancing our logic and emotions. How can you "turn down the volume" on your emotions so you can make better money decisions? Here are several techniques to help you do just that.

Before you make a large purchase or sign the loan document… stop and breathe! Ask yourself, "How am I feeling right now?" Close your eyes, get quiet, and listen to your body. If you're feeling anything other than positive and peaceful, put down the credit card and take a step back. Are you feeling sad, bored, angry, fearful, lonely, or something else? Is your emotional volume loud right now? Don't fight against the emotion or stuff it down. Find a healthy way to let the emotion move through your body. If you're feeling angry, get in a good sweaty kickboxing workout. If you're sad, watch Bambi or The Notebook and let yourself cry a river about other people's sad stories. (A fabulous suggestion from my mentor, Melanie Ann Layer.) If you're lonely, call your elderly relative or visit them in person. If you're bored, sign up for a painting class or volunteer at the local animal shelter. Identify the feelings and healthy ways to fulfill the emotional needs that require little to no money.

One of my past clients, Jenni, noticed that her online shopping sprees occurred immediately after her phone calls with her overly critical mother. She felt demoralized when she hung up the phone, and online shopping gave her the hit of dopamine she craved. Once we identified her trigger, I asked her to come up with a list of ten no-cost things she could do to make herself feel good. Her list included calling her best friend, taking a walk outside in nature with her husband, petting her cats, taking a bubble bath, and making herself a cup of her favorite tea. Jenni posted her list next to her computer monitor with this written at the top: "Feeling stressed or depressed? Try one of these before you shop." She made a deal with herself that she would do one of the things on her "Feel Good" list before she shopped online. Guess what? She decreased her spending online by 70% with this simple technique.

Another strategy for turning down your emotional volume is to wait 24 hours before making a major financial decision. About 99% of the time, our money situations don't require immediate action from us. My husband and I always wait at least a day before major purchase decisions like buying cars or real estate. You and your partner might want to set a dollar threshold for the 24-hour waiting period. For example, you could decide to wait overnight on any purchase over $500 or $1,000. Don't allow high-pressure tactics from commissioned salespeople to rush you into a buying decision. My ex-fiancé was a used car salesman, so I know all of their tricks, like saying, "This is the last one in stock" or "Someone else is coming by to look at it later today, so you better buy it now." Sleeping on the decision naturally allows you to come down from the "buyer's high" and evaluate the purchase both logically and emotionally. If the numbers make sense for your financial situation and you feel positive and peaceful, go ahead and buy it.

If you're facing a complicated financial situation fraught with emotion, it's wise to bring in outside help. If you're experiencing divorce or widowhood, waiting 24 hours isn't going to be enough to decrease your emotional volume when you're going through an extended shitstorm of a situation. Employ the services of a financial coach, advisor, or CPA with plenty of experience leading people through your situation. When I'm coaching a client who's lost their spouse via death or divorce, I guide them step by step through the fog of emotions. Together, we're making wise financial decisions that they'll be happy with both now and later. At the very least, consult a money-wise friend or family member to talk through important financial decisions.

Before you make a major money move, stop and take a deep breath. Are you feeling positive and peaceful? If not, identify what emotions you're feeling. Are you trying to self-soothe with money? If so, stop and do something that will help you move the emotions through your body in a healthy way. Wait 24 hours for your emotional volume to quiet down. Seek out an objective opinion from a financial professional or the money-smart person in your life. It's not about deprivation; it's about untangling your emotions from money so you can make intentional decisions that honor both your inner Provider King and Pleasure Queen!

Chapter Eighteen

Celebrating Financial Success

If you achieve a major milestone, like paying off your student loans or getting a huge raise, do you shout it from the rooftops? Most of us are not comfortable talking privately about money, much less sharing publicly about our financial successes. I'd love for this to change, and see people celebrating their money wins the same way they share their sweaty 5K selfies and bicep flexes at the gym. At the end of every year, I compare our financial situation to the previous year. How has our net worth changed? How have our investments grown? What financial milestones did we achieve? Sometimes, from week to week, month to month, the improvements aren't quite as obvious as reviewing yearly progress.

In 2019, I felt disheartened about my finances because I'd had two dismal profit years in my business. These were my sixth and seventh years working full-time in my business. I berated myself because I felt by now I should have "arrived." But as most business owners know, success is rarely a straight line. Imagine my surprise when I conducted our annual financial review and discovered that Nick and I had a net worth of over one million dollars! It was official. We were millionaires. *Wait... what?* Wasn't I supposed to feel different now? Where was the falcon delivering my invitation to the golf country club, Harry Potter-style? Shouldn't someone be throwing us a party at a mansion with champagne and caviar?

Instead, the whole thing felt anticlimactic. Who could I even tell who wouldn't think I was showing off or rubbing it in their face? Crickets. Besides sharing the news with Nick, who doesn't like sharing his personal business with anyone, I said nothing. I did nothing to celebrate or mark the pretty damn momentous occasion. It wasn't until several years later, in a mastermind with a multi-millionaire mentor, that I finally had a community of like-minded women with whom I could freely share my financial successes. We joyfully celebrated each other's money wins, whether earned or gifted.

Now, I make a point to celebrate my financial successes, sometimes privately and sometimes publicly. In 2021, my husband and I paid off our mortgage and became 100% debt-free. I celebrated that money win loud and proud! And some people took offense at my celebration. Some people told me that I shouldn't share my money wins because it makes other people feel ashamed of their financial situation. Other people told me I should have kept my mortgage and instead invested the money. Thankfully, most people simply celebrated with me! The reason many of us hesitate to share our financial wins is the fear of what other people will think of us. Will they think we're bragging? Will they think we don't deserve it?

When you have a financial gain in Provider energy, there is a sense of having earned it. You worked hard and got the promotion. You disciplined yourself to pay off all of your credit cards. You put your nose to the grindstone and achieved a record profit year in your business. There is a sense of accomplishment because you earned it. Sometimes, those victories are easier to celebrate because they are won through sweat and effort. When you have a financial gain in Pleasure energy, there's a sense of miracles and wonder. A major corporation offers you millions to license your trademark. Your ninety-eight-year-old great-aunt leaves you her jewelry collection worth a small fortune. You win $10,000 on a scratch-off lottery ticket. Sometimes, these victories are easier to celebrate because they feel like luck and magic.

Which financial wins are easier for you to celebrate? Those earned in Provider energy or those miraculously received in Pleasure energy? It's worth examining your discomfort over money wins and celebration in general. I encourage you to think about how you want to celebrate your financial progress moving forward. Your celebrations don't have to be publicly announced on social media, but they certainly can be. Maybe it's more your style to have a special celebration meal at a five-star restaurant with your friend, partner, or immediate family. If you don't have anyone you feel comfortable bragging to, please reach out to me on social media, and we'll celebrate virtually together!

Chapter Nineteen

Relationships and Money

Now that you've evaluated and reflected on your personal relationship with the Provider and Pleasure energies of money, let's talk about money management in relationships. This is where it gets messy. Each partner brings to the relationship their unique emotional money baggage, unconscious patterns, and inherited biases when it comes to thinking, feeling, and relating to money. Money is like sex. Most of us were never formally taught how to do it, yet we're expected to be good at it. But it's also not polite to talk about it. No wonder so many people have a dysfunctional relationship with money! Then we couple up and hope our financial dysfunctions balance each other out (which rarely happens).

If your Pleasure Queen rules your financial kingdom, you might seek a partner with strong Provider King energy. Unfortunately, it's not a case where two halves make a whole. In fact, it might create an even more unbalanced situation that creates a high level of conflict. Married couples who are in this dynamic seek me out for coaching. One partner feels overburdened with financial responsibility, and the other partner feels that they're being scolded by a parent for having any measure of fun with money. The key to managing money well as a couple is both partners' willingness to improve financial habits and money mindset. Exploring and discussing your past experiences with money in an open and non-judgmental way is a wonderful place to start. *"How did your parents handle money? Do you agree with their approach?"* Asking these questions can be extremely eye-opening and deepen your understanding of your partner's money story.

If you're legally married, you and your spouse are 50/50 financial partners in the joint venture known as Your Marriage, Inc. So, how do you handle the division of labor when it comes to managing the household finances? Honestly, it's a very individualized decision. But here's what I know doesn't work: one person being 100% responsible for the finances and the other person being 0% responsible.

When one person has all the control and responsibility in the relationship, it creates fertile ground for dysfunction and conflict. You and your partner should discuss each of your money management preferences, strengths, and weaknesses. If you're a natural "numbers person," you might not mind (and even enjoy) taking charge of updating the personal finance app and paying household bills. If your spouse is intrigued with the stock market and crypto, they might want to take the lead with your investments.

If neither of you has adequate money management aptitude, it's time to hire a financial coach or take a personal finance course together (see the Reflection Journal for recommendations). Wise money management is a skill, not a character trait. It can be learned! We all have the capacity to be sensible money managers. What we might lack is competence and confidence. To be competent with money, you need a combination of financial wisdom, emotional intelligence, and practice, practice, practice. If you want to excel at playing the piano, you need both instruction and many hours of practice. Why would we expect personal finance to be any different? Confidence in your money management naturally flourishes as your competence increases.

In my household, as you might imagine, I take the lead on the day-to-day financial management. It's not that my husband can't do it. He's always been an excellent money manager. It's more because I enjoy doing it! I ensure our expenses are properly classified in our personal finance app and pay the bills out of our joint checking account (most are on autopay). Nick and I have regular discussions regarding unusual expenses, taxes, and investments. I insist we're both involved with all meetings with our Money Team (financial planner, tax accountant, and attorney). If, God forbid, something happened to me, I want Nick to feel confident stepping in and taking over the money management.

Keep in mind that your shared financial responsibilities in a committed partnership can change over time. If your spouse gets a new job that requires frequent travel, he or she might not be the best person to be responsible for the day-to-day financial management anymore. If one of you is battling an illness or caring for an aging parent, the other partner might need to step in and take more responsibility for managing your joint personal finances. I highly recommend that couples read my book *Money Is Emotional: Prevent Your Heart from Hijacking Your Wallet* together (or listen to the Money Is Emotional podcast). Doing so creates natural conversations around the nuances of personal finance and the emotional side of money.

What if you're nervous about even starting the conversation around money? Kevin Bruce Scott, Men's Empowerment and Relationship Coach, suggests having a pre-conversation before talking about money. He suggests saying something like this, "Okay, let's both take a deep breath. We're going to figure out talking about money together, and we're going to make it fun. *Do you want to do that? Yes?* Okay. This is also going to be uncomfortable, especially at first. *Are you ready? Yes?* Okay. If you get angry, or if I get angry, we're not leaving the relationship. Can we agree on that?" If you set the stage for your money conversations in this way, you're vastly increasing your chances for a positive outcome.

Chapter Twenty

The Balancing Act

The act of balancing the roles of the Provider King and the Pleasure Queen energies in your finances is more art than science. It's not a matter of trying to achieve a perfect blend of each because that's nearly impossible for several reasons. Life circumstances are in a constant state of flux, and many of these things affect your money. Some circumstances are within your control, and others are not. Your mother-in-law might get divorced and move into your home temporarily, which results in extra expenses for your family. Your boss might promote you and give you a big, fat raise. The only constant we can expect in our finances is change!

It's like surfing in the ocean. The water is continually shifting beneath your surfboard. It's up to you to shift your body in response to what's going on around you and underneath you to stay upright. A newbie surfer puts all of their concentration on stabilizing themselves so they can remain on the board instead of in the water. A skilled surfer reads the waves and anticipates what's coming toward them. Stability on the board is second nature because of their thousands of hours of experience. The surfer sees a terrifyingly high wave as a potential opportunity for a thrilling ride because they know how to use the force of it for their own advantage.

When you first attempt to keep the balance of Provider and Pleasure Money, you will feel like a newbie surfer struggling to find some stability. This is normal and part of the process. It's easy to look at others who are navigating their finances like a pro surfer and feel envious or imagine they're just lucky. Most started in a very similar spot, on shaky legs like a newborn fawn.

When your Provider energy is solid, you're informed and in control of your money. You're the boss! You feel safe and secure, confident in your financial future. You know you can't foresee all possible doomsday scenarios, which is why you have a margin for error built into your finances. When your Pleasure energy is optimized, you are fully enjoying the present while looking forward to the future. You savor your intentional pleasure purchases and add new thrilling adventures and treasures to your vision board. You have enough margin in your money for generosity and spontaneity. Your emotions around your finances are primarily positive and peaceful.

When I speak of balancing Provider and Pleasure Money, it doesn't mean that your income and spending are a 50/50 split in terms of amounts. We go through certain phases of life, and even times of the year, when there's an emphasis on one or the other. You can think of it like phases of the moon, which are constantly shifting between light, dark, and a balance of the two. On any given day, you're flowing in and out of both energies. Provider and Pleasure energies are like the yin and yang symbol, except it's not a flat two-dimensional circle. It's more like a 3-D sphere with the two energies swirling inside with constant movement. Where they meet, there isn't a distinct dividing line but rather a blending at the edges of the energies into each other. Provider and Pleasure energies are like two sides of the money coin. If you look at the edge, can you tell where one side begins and the other one ends?

Money management is an art, not a science. However, many personal finance gurus are happy to give you the exact formulas that worked wonders for them. Beware of adopting someone else's money system verbatim as your own. Honestly, that's the easy way out. If it doesn't work, then you can simply blame the guru (or yourself) for its failure. You will find that your financial management system changes and evolves as you learn, grow, and change. You'll need to flex your approach as you move through different life stages and events. Money management is about both the logical and the emotional, the structure and the flow, the responsibility and the fun, the systems and the spontaneity.

Ideally, your Provider King and Pleasure Queen will be ruling side by side, complementing and supporting each other to create a financial kingdom that is both architecturally sound and a work of art.

ENJOY THIS BOOK? YOU CAN MAKE A BIG DIFFERENCE!

I'm so grateful for my committed and loyal readers! Your reviews are one of the best thank-yous I can receive. Reviews are the most powerful tool I have as an author when it comes to bringing my books to the attention of other readers.

If you enjoyed this book, I would be grateful if you could spend three minutes leaving a review (it can be as short as you like) on the book's Amazon page. Please and thank you!

WEALTHY WOMAN BOOK CLUB™

Join us in the Wealthy Woman Book Club™, where the book is just the beginning!

The beginning of what?

Increased financial intelligence

Exploration and lively discussion

Critical thinking about your money

Greater awareness of your unconscious patterns

A community that encourages you - and holds you accountable

And a whole lot of FUN!!

And yes, the Wealthy Woman Book Club™ is for YOU, no matter your income, age, or financial experience level.

Scan the code with your phone's camera app to join us today!

Also By Christine Luken

Money is Emotional: Prevent Your Heart from Hijacking Your Wallet

If money is emotional, then why do we persist in trying to manage our personal finances logically? We already know what it takes to become financially healthy: spend less than we make, pay down our debt, and save more money. Money management books, tools, and techniques abound, yet most of us don't utilize them. Maybe you've adopted the practice of ignoring money problems until they are barreling down on you like a tidal wave, as I once did. I know what it feels like to be drowning financially.

I'd like to propose a better alternative, one that doesn't require you to eat beans and rice or to spend hours updating budget spreadsheets. My approach to personal finance is called "Mindful Money Management." It is unique in that it harnesses the power of your emotions so they can propel you forward like a rocket booster toward your Preferred Financial Destination. Yes, money is emotional, but you can prevent your heart from hijacking your wallet. Let me show you how. Available from Amazon and Audible. Download the first three chapters at: https://www.christineluken.com/books/

Manage Money Like a Boss: A Financial Guide for Creative Entrepreneurs

You're doing what you love for a living, making a business out of your creativity, whether it's photography, fashion, music, marketing, writing, or crafting the perfect microbrew.

The only problem? Managing your business finances is a serious drag. Accounting is confusing. Taxes are scary. And most financial experts you know are intimidating. (Are they speaking another language?)

You deserve financial guidance that's simple to understand and implement, from someone who honors and appreciates your creativity. As both a writer and an accountant, I love both words and numbers. I will demystify money for you so it can become your best employee, rather than your worst nightmare.

This isn't just a book about business finance. We dive deep into some surprising things that impact your bottom line, to help you make more money, get more customers, and look like a pro. I will give you both the confidence and competence to manage your money like a BOSS. Available from Amazon. Download the first three chapters at: https://www.christineluken.com/books/

Financial Dignity After Divorce: A Woman's Guide to Healing her Relationship with Money

Ready to recover a positive and peaceful relationship with your money? You might be feeling alone, overwhelmed, and confused about handling money (and life) on your own after divorce. You might even feel like a failure at having to start over. I know because I've been there, too!

If you're experiencing money shame or anxiety due to the breakup of your marriage or long-term relationship, Financial Dignity® After Divorce will empower you to recover a positive and peaceful relationship with your money.

This book is designed to help divorcing women like you to:

- Increase your financial security
- Identify & defuse your emotional money hot buttons
- Manage your personal finances with ease and certainty
- Release the money baggage from your previous relationship
- Develop healthy money behaviors to carry you confidently into the future

Money is like the third person in your marriage. But unlike your ex, you and money will be together forever! Money wants to support your happiness, not stress you out. In this book, you'll discover the step-by-step process to effectively manage both your emotions and your money so you can walk confidently into your bright future. Available from Amazon and Audible. Download the first three chapters at: https://www.christineluken.com/books/

FINANCIAL DIGNITY® COURSES BY CHRISTINE LUKEN

Increase Financial Dignity® at your own pace!

Christine Luken offers value-packed, on-demand courses for improving all areas of your money.

Whether you want to create a Magnetic Money Mindset, manage your business finances like a boss, clear your emotional money triggers, or learn Christine's complete Financial Dignity® system for your personal finances, there's something for you at:

https://www.christineluken.com/courses/

About the Author

Ready for money to support your happiness rather than stress you out? Then you need Christine Luken, Financial Dignity® Coach, in your corner!

As the Founder of the Financial Dignity® Movement, Christine has coached hundreds of high-earning professionals, business owners, and divorcing women to pay off staggering amounts of debt and massively increase their net worth. The author of four books and host of the Wealthy Woman Book Club™, Christine blends wise money management with emotional intelligence.

When she's not connecting with her global online community or recording an episode of the Money is Emotional podcast from her office in beautiful Kentucky, you can find her on the golf course, by the pool, or curled up with a good book, a fluffy cat, and a strong cup of coffee. Christine can be reached on her website: www.ChristineLuken.com

Acknowledgments

Here are the people in my circle who deserve a special Thank You for supporting me in the writing and publishing of this book.

My Circle of 8: Carissa, Tammy, Heather, Margo, Camilla, Marie, and Elizabeth. Thank you for being my magical manifesting besties!

My spiritual mentors who have walked alongside me and guided me to the fullness of myself: Nicole Casteel, Casandra Austin-McDonald, Sarah Belle, and Juliette Karaman-van Schaardenburg.

Heather Hutzel, what can I say? *Seriously, thank you for EVERYTHING!*

Gwenette Gaddis, my editor, for taming my punctuation into submission.

My Alpha Readers, Leah Jetter and Nicholle Bays, thank you for your invaluable input, friendship, and support!

Finally, a big THANK YOU to all of my family, friends, and followers who supported me in some way during the writing and publishing of this book! Please know I am eternally grateful for your love and support!

Made in United States
North Haven, CT
10 November 2026

22095623R00088